D1494312

Bitey
the
Vegie VAMPIRE

ɓ APR

OCT 200

RY

Bitey the Veggie **VAMPIRE**

And Other Weird Poems for Wacky Children

by

Chris White

The King's England Press
2000

ISBN 1 872438 67 9

Bitey the Veggie Vampire is typeset by Moose Manuscripts in
Futura Casual 17pt and published by
The King's England Press Ltd,
Cambertown House, Commercial Road, Goldthorpe,
Rotherham, South Yorkshire, S63 9BL

Printed and bound in Great Britain by

Woolnough Bookbinding
Irthlingborough
Northamptonshire

Foreword

This book has been 15 years in the making! Although I have been drawing pretty much non-stop for all that time it has always been for other people. One day I realised I had nothing for myself.

So, during boring school lessons, long days at work, train journeys and those quiet moments when your mind wanders, these poems were scribbled down and shoved in a drawer.

When that drawer wouldn't shut any more I wondered if anyone out there would like to share them with me.

That's where the fine people at The King's England Press came in. Although I sometimes think I'm dreaming, here are those scribbles, dusted down and spruced up just for you.

I think what I'm trying to say is that if you get one of those quiet, mind-wandering moments, grab a pen and paper quick. Look what can happen!

This book is for
my mum and dad - thanks for everything.
Also, cheers to Paula,
the biggest, baddest sister to walk the earth.

Bitey, the Veggie Vampire

Bitey was a vampire,
Who wasn't very good.
He couldn't stand the taste of meat
Or the smell of blood.

Whilst his vampire friends ran wild in the dark,
Bitey could not find his niche.
As they bit necks and ate human flesh,
Bitey just fancied some quiche.

The outfit was right, the gothic clothes,
It was Halloween when he was born.
If only the necks he was meant to devour
Were made from a nice piece of quorn.

Bitey tried to be evil,
To cause a bit more of a fright,
So off he set, fangs glistening,
Into the summer's night...

When the sun rose, though, the truth became clear,
Bitey had not left his mark.
The most daring act he'd committed all night?
He ate a parsnip in the dark!

The other vampires just laughed at him,
None of them understood,
That even if Bitey grazed his own knee
He'd faint at the sight of his blood.

"But my diet's healthy!" he protested.
"I feel fine, and, I suppose,
I save money on dry cleaning
With no blood-stains on my clothes."

Alas, Bitey's story does not finish well,
It does not finish well at all,
For the malfunctioning vampire's aversion to meat
Was, in the end, his downfall.

You see Bitey was slain, it was just last week
When his whole world fell apart.
He was found late at night, when the moon was bright,
With a 12 ounce steak through his heart.

Something Smelly

There's something smelly in the fridge,
Is it cheese or some other fare?
No, I'm afraid the dog is dead,
So I went and stuffed him in there!

Never Give a Duck a Pen

Never give a duck a pen,
Decline him, without being rude,
For although it looks like he wants to write,
He really just thinks that it's food.

But give a pen to a monkey,
And, with a bit of luck,
Give him just a few days and he'll
Probably write this book!

11

My Hamster

My hamster's only got one eye
In the middle of his head.
He just sits there and stares at me
As I get ready for bed.

And when I walk around my room
I somehow still can feel
His hamster eye fixed right on me
Even though he's on his wheel.

At night-time when all proper pets
Towards sleep should be heading,
I still can see his beady eye
Peeping through his bedding.

I think next time I get one
I'll make sure that mum buys
One that's a little nicer
And has got both of its eyes!

Stumpy

He's only got one little leg,
His feathers are matted and lumpy,
He's the mankiest pigeon you ever did see
And he goes by the name of Stumpy.

His beak is blunt, his eyes are dull,
His wings are weak and frail,
His breath smells of unpleasant things
And there's pigeon pooh on his tail.

Stumpy lives in the market place
With his pigeon friends,
They spend all day hunting for chips
Amongst the old fag ends.

"How come one leg?" I hear you ask.
It's because he was hit by a cab
Whilst trying to cross the inner ring road
To eat a discarded kebab.

1809 — 1883

He'll sit with his pals on the top of statues
But if one of them should cough,
Stumpy, because of his lack of both legs,
Will more than likely fall off.

Because Stumpy can't run very fast
And it's such an effort to fly,
He'll be left bruised and battered
'Cause someone has kicked him as they walked by.

Even though most pigeons are just one big pain
That always get in the way
Stumpy's not like that, he's not like the rest,
He's the one pigeon that's okay.

So the next time you're out in the City
And you see a bird that's a bit jumpy,
Don't run and shout "Shoo!", see if his legs number two
'Cause it might be the one they call Stumpy.

Octopus Jim

Octopus Jim is a popular guy,
He's got friend after friend,
But keeping in touch with all of them
Drives him round the bend.

The ocean is so very big,
With so many places to be
That with all the fishy friends Jim's got,
There's too many to see in the sea.

But now Jim can stay in touch with his mates
Without even leaving his home:
He took some birthday money he'd saved
And bought eight mobile phones.

Gordon

Gordon was a tiny flea
Who had trouble every year.
You see his family was so big,
Buying presents was quite dear.

He had four hundred siblings,
That's a birthday every day.
So when time came to get them gifts
He couldn't afford to pay.

But this year it's not so expensive,
'Cause of the shop he found.
Now his brothers and sisters each get a gift from
'Everything's A Pound'.

Nigel and Frank

Nigel the frog was in need of a snog
To turn him into a prince.
But it wasn't a joke that he had a high croak
And walked with a bit of a mince.

Girl frogs were just not appealing, but he did get a tingly fee
Whenever his friend Frank hopped by,
And he really enjoyed the evenings they'd spend,
Sucking on a fly.

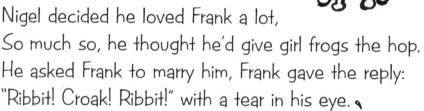

Nigel decided he loved Frank a lot,
So much so, he thought he'd give girl frogs the hop.
He asked Frank to marry him, Frank gave the reply:
"Ribbit! Croak! Ribbit!" with a tear in his eye.

It was the finest frog wedding you've ever seen,
The groom looked great and the bride wore green.
They were joined together by a newt called Roy
And both the frogs jumped for joy.

The day worked out so perfectly,
The food, the guests, the weather,
Then Nigel and Frank left for the river-bank
Where they moved into a pad together.

Dog Nap

Dog lay in his basket,
His blanket kept him warm.
He'd had a tiring morning
Digging up the lawn.

Doggy eyelids slowly drooped
Until he could not keep
His weary doggy body
From drifting off to sleep.

"I could be in the movies,"
Dog began to dream,
"And win lots of awards and things
For acting on the screen."

"I could be a secret agent,
Yeah, that would be nice.
Confronting Dr Tibbles
And his evil clockwork mice."

"Or maybe I'd be a huge monst
With an ultra-sonic roar.
I'd crush entire cities
Under one gigantic paw."

"Yes, this film would be the one for me,
A pacey action-thriller.
The people on the streets would cry,
'Look out! Here comes Dogzilla!'

"Or maybe aboard a great big boat
I could meet another dog.
We'd fall in love and sail the seas
(And maybe have a snog!)."

"I'd squeeze her paw upon the deck
And then I'd squeeze it twice.
This film would be unsinkable
(If we just watched out for ice)."

"But then I could make my audience laugh
In a comedy role,
By chewing on a rubber bone
Or falling in my bowl."

"I'd go to a very important event
And how the crowd would cheer,
As I made my way to collect the award
For *The Funniest Dog of the Year.*"

"I could be in the movie,
I could be an award winner.
But it is so warm here in my basket
And it's nearly time for dinner."

"Maybe tomorrow," Dog thought,
"Or maybe the day after that."
Then flopped out of his basket
And went to chase a cat.

Harold

Harold was a slippery snake
Who always shed his skin.
Every month he got a new
Body to live in.

He had so many empty suits,
Do you know what he did?
He took them to a car boot sale
And made almost nine quid.

Henry

Henry was a caterpillar,
The nicest you could meet,
He had a long, green body
And lots of tiny feet.

But although he was quite hairy,
I'm afraid it must be told,
He had no hair upon his head,
He was completely bald.

Henry tried so many ways
To hide his lack of hair:
A scarf, a hat, forget all that,
His scalp was still threadbare.

Henry knew what must be done
So he took a trip one day,
Withdrew all his savings from the bank
And bought a big toupee.

Centipedes swooned and fleas fainted,
Henry's now a lady-killer.
He's known wood-wide as the wonderful
Wiggy, wiggly caterpillar.

Babies

There's a baby in a pram on the path over there,
Being pushed where he doesn't want to go.
He's zipped up in a coat and under a hat,
With only his eyes on show.

Doesn't he feel like just shouting, "Stop!
I don't want to go this way!
And how about letting me choose what I want
To wear when we're out for the day!"

Why don't they scream, "LIBERATION!
Stop pushing me around - I can walk!"
Why don't they rise and scream, "LET US BE FREE!"
I s'pose it's 'cause babies can't talk!

My Dog

My dog has only got one leg,
But apart from that he's fine.
He can lick like other dogs,
And bark and growl and whine.
And if you scratch his tummy
His tail will start to wag,
You just can't take him for a walk,
You take him for a drag.

Terence

Terence the duck was right out of luck
When it came to swimming too well.
As the people on land threw bread from their hand,
Terence would go through sheer hell.

His friends would see bread and leave him for dead,
With a whoosh and a splash they'd be there.
But try though he must to get one soggy crust,
His meal-times were getting quite rare.

So one day Terence thought, "I know what must be bought,"
And went to the shop on the shore.
With a cheque that he wrote, he bought a speedboat,
And didn't go hungry anymore.

Ted's Bad Dream

If you give me a moment to set the scene,
I'll tell you the story of Ted's bad dream...

'Twas the night before Thursday
And all through the house
Not a creature was stirring,
Except Ted the mouse.

He couldn't get thirty,
Never mind forty winks,
So he fluffed up his pillow
And laid back to think...

He thought of his bed,
And the wall over there.
"I'm safe and secure
And don't have a care."

But then Ted thought harde
Sat up and yawned,
And thought about life
Beyond his skirting-board...

His mind slowly wandered
To the friends that he had,
And how just lately
They looked kind of sad.

Take Kim the cow
And what she had to say:
"I stand in my field
And eat food all day."

"But every so often
I lean down for grass,
And spit out a can
Or a sharp piece of glass."

"While I'm eating my dinner
It makes my teeth judder.
Do you think I can eat it?
No way! Pull the udder!"

"We should look after the countryside,
And keep our eyes peeled.
Put cans and glass where they belong,
In a bin, not my field."

Back in his mousehole
Ted lay in bed
When his old friend the Fish
Swam into his head.

"I spend my days in this riv
Just swimming up and dow
It used to be a sparkling bl
But now it's murky brown."

"There's a rusty bike, old car tyres,
Occasionally nuclear waste.
New things are dumped here every day,
I'm surprised I'm not fish paste."

TOXIC

"There was a time I had some friends,
With plants and life down here.
But that was before the poison and pain,
Back when the view was clear."

"When I think of what humans have done
It makes my scales quiver.
This isn't a bin to throw your junk in,
It's meant to be home, it's my river."

FOR SALE

Meanwhile in the hole
Ted lay in bed
And his old friend the bird
Flew into his head.

"Way up here you would think
I'd be safe from man down there.
I'd fly through the sky, head held high,
Breathing clean, fresh air."

"I used to have not a care in the world,
Chirping my songs out loud.
Now the buildings and factories below
Send me thick, black cloud."

"Most of the time I can't see a thing,
Surrounded by pollution and smoke.
I've seen starlings cough, blackbirds gasp,
It's got beyond a joke."

"If only some of the factories would stop,
I'm sure the rest would follow.
It used to be so refreshing up here,
Now I can hardly swallow."

Meanwhile in the hole
Ted was sweating in bed
As his old pal the Dog
Leapt into his head.

"I love to scamper down the streets
And run about the place.
That is until a gust of wind
Blows paper in my face."

"It's great to go out for a walk
On my master's lead.
We walk for hours, never stop
(Only when I've peed)."

"Now, when I look down the street
What is it I see?
Pavements of litter, broken glass,
Walls of graffiti."

"My master often comments
How it all looks rather sad.
But if glass on the floor cut his paw,
He'd be barking mad!"

Back in his hole
Ted rolled out of bed,
Fell to the floor
And banged his head.

Ted woke up and looked around,
Then sat up with a start,
An aching feeling in his head,
A pounding in his heart.

The mouse stared out across the room,
The sweat started to stream.
He looked around, there was no sound,
"Thank goodness! Just a dream!"

He knew mankind would never get
Itself in such a state,
Killing creatures, polluting the earth,
Not knowing it's too late.

Ted thought to himself, "Just in case,
There's something I must do."
He knelt by his bed and prayed in his head
That not all dreams come true.

Something Smells

"Something smells. What can it be?"
Little Bobby said.
"Is it me, or is it you?"
"Nope - the gerbil's dead!"

T.V.

There's nothing on the t.v., ever, ever, ever!
Just soaps and tacky talk shows
And forecasts on the weather.
Why don't people just switch off
If they're not happy with what they're seeing?
Go outside,
See the world
And be a human being!

Dragon For Hire

If I said I knew of a dragon,
Who was friendly and not at all bad.
If I told you I knew of a dragon,
Would you tell me that I was quite mad?

I'll do my best to tell you his story:
I think he was short and quite podgy,
Some of my memories are sketchy you see,
And some of my rhyming is dodgy!

I know he was born all alone in the world,
Not hatched into titles or wealth.
His mother and father were nowhere around,
So he had to look after himself.

As the dragon thought of his purpose in life,
And down what path he'd be led,
He let out a cough, flames shot from his jaws,
And burnt down a small cowshed.

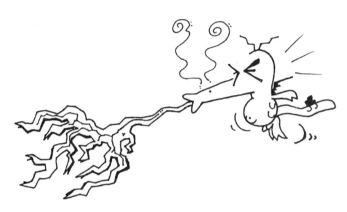

"Holy smoke!" the dragon screamed,
"Where did that come from?"
Then realised he'd been given a gift,
And a very useful one.

"I know now what I must do:
Go forth and create fire.
People will flock from miles around
When they see *Dragon For Hire*.

45

So the dragon set off walking,
To see what jobs he could find.
Something quite glamorous, well-paid and well-loved
Were the things he had in mind.

He'd not been walking for too long,
when he came across a town,
and running towards him was a man waving,
a sausage up and down.

He shouted, "I've got all the family round,
But I don't know what I'm gonna do!
They're sat in my garden with empty stomachs and plate
'Cause I can't light my barbecue!

"Aha!" thought the dragon. "Here's my big chance!"
He stood, legs astride, and took aim...
Not only did the barbie light,
The whole garden went up in flames!

"Stop that dragon!" Aunt Nelly yelled.
"Frank! Go call the cops!"
But the dragon had scarpered down the street
In a shower of black pork chops.

"Not to worry!" the dragon thought,
"I'll get it right next time.
There must be someone that can use
This fantastic gift of mine."

"Hey! Over here!" the cry came
And the dragon spun around.
He saw two men under a balloon
That couldn't get off the ground.

"We're trying to get this thing moving,
We want to be up there.
You wouldn't be a darling, would you,
And lend us your hot air?"

Dragon stepped into the basket
And blew with all his might.
An orange flame warmed the air,
The balloon slowly took flight...

Up they went into the sky,
Slowly getting higher.
Everything went well until
The balloon went and caught fire!

There was much plummeting and shouting.
Dragon knew he had made a mistake
When they yelled, "Get lost, Scaly! You're useless!"
From the middle of a lake.

Undeterred, the dragon strolled on,
Feeling quite alone,
When a few yards down the street he saw
A frozen old folks home.

"Our boiler's broken," the old man said.
"We sit down to have a natter,
But it's so cold in there, I swear,
If we had teeth, they'd chatter!"

The dragon surveyed the boiler
And it looked ever so old.
But he just couldn't leave the folks here
To play dominoes in the cold.

He took a pipe into his mouth,
Held it with a paw,
And heat soared through the frosted pipes,
The room began to thaw.

"One more puff should do it!"
The old folks all cried, "No!
The boiler's so old, if you heat it some more
The whole place is gonna blow!"

"Too late!" shouted someone, and there was a BOOM!
That shattered the double glazing.
Everywhere you looked cardigans were cut,
And war blazers were blazing.

"Get out!" cried the old folks, catching their breath,
"You're no use to anyone!"
And as walking sticks waved and boiled sweets were hurled
In a puff of smoke he was gone.

And that's how I remember the story,
Of a dragon that must be admired,
For persisting to share his fire with the world,
Even though it kept getting him fired!

And that is why we think the last dragon died out,
There was nothing for him to do.
So if you've got a talent, make sure that it's used,
Or the same thing may happen to you!

John Wallaby

John Wallaby loved to play golf,
He thought the game was neat,
But got quite chilly on the course,
Especially round his feet.

So his wife (the lovely Wilma)
Knitted some socks for John,
But when he got on the golf course
He got a hole in one.

The Man on the Train

There's a man that sits on the train with me
Who has a black brief-case.
He sits in the same seat everyday,
And has an evil face.

He often glances at me
And his eyes burn into mine.
You can sometimes hear him mumbling
That the train is not on time.

As I sit there in a morning
Thoughts always come to me.
Just what exactly is within
The brief-case on his knee?

On a Monday it's maybe a monster,
With horns and a mouth like a funnel,
That he uses to suck up small children
Whenever we go through a tunnel.

On a Tuesday I think it's a tentacle
That unravels itself for a mile,
Then grabs the ticket conductor's leg
And drags him down the aisle.

On Wednesday I wonder if it's a wolf
That leaps out of the case with a wail!
It slobbers on the man next to me, then
Bites a hole in his *Daily Mail.*

On Thursday I'm thinking that there is a thing
That came from outer space.
It followed a lady into the loo
And she came out with spots on her face.

On Friday I fear that a few hundred fish
Spill out onto the floor,
And they make such a smell on the platform outside
When the train opens its door.

I'm afraid I can't tell you if the weekend's the same,
Because on Saturday and Sunday I don't get the train.

I think that the man is suspicious
As he keeps glaring at me,
And I think that he knows that I think, in his case,
Is something I'm not meant to see.

But I'm sure it's only papers and files
That the brief-case holds inside.
But I think I prefer my version of things,
It makes for a less boring ride!

Never Feed Ducks Jelly Babies

Never feed ducks jelly babies,
It makes them mad and see red.
It's because they have no teeth in their beaks
To bite off their little heads.

And never feed ducks garlic bread,
It always makes them wish
They'd not had it the night before,
'Cause they can't creep up on fish.

And never feed ducks hamburgers,
Not even for a treat.
It's not easy picking gherkins out
When you've only got webbed feet!

But never, ever, ever
Give ducks fine cheese and wine
'Cause they develop quite a taste for it
And then have it all the time.

The Bear in my Wardrobe

There's a bear that lives in my wardrobe,
He keeps trying on my clothes.
He pulls on my shirt and jumper,
Wipes my hanky on his nose.
My trousers he'll yank over his stubby legs,
Tries socks on pair after pair.
Sometimes he'll fling the doors open wide
And run round in my underwear.

The bear I have no objection to,
Even though I think he's insane,
It's just that after he's tried my clothes on
Nothing fits me again.

Simon

Simon was a worker ant,
He worked and worked all day,
Lifting stones twice his height
With never time to play.

One morning Simon woke and thought,
"I don't fancy work today."
So he rang in sick and took his wife
On a skiing holiday.

Gerald the Pig

Not so long ago,
On a farm not far away,
Was a large grassy field
Where the piglets used to play.

Now the piglets had no worries,
They played there all the day,
Only stopping after dark
To lie back in the hay.

The sun would rise and so would they
To play another game,
All except one tiny pig -
Gerald was his name.

Gerald was a puzzled pig,
He thought these games were good,
But couldn't bring himself each day
To roll round in the mud.

Gerald would stand and watch his friends
As they frollicked in the sludge,
But thought, "There's better things to do,"
And to the barn he trudged.

There he sat and pondered,
And thoughts flashed through his mind...
"There must be more to life than this,
And more I'm going to find!"

One night he left his friends asleep
And quietly trotted out,
With two apples, a pear, a comb for his hair
And a hanky for his snout.

The city lights grew brighter,
And Gerald finally knew
There'd be no mud in the city,
And lots of things to do.

He looked and looked for something
He thought he might enjoy.
Soon he saw a circus tent
And Gerald thought, "Oh, boy!"

They put him on the trapeze,
Where he could swing around,
But the poor young pig lost his grip
And fell straight to the ground.

Gerald missed the safety net
And landed with a thud,
Not safely on the floor,
But in a patch of mud.

So Gerald left the circus,
(He didn't like the mud),
And saw a football stadium
And thought, "That might be good."

The team put Gerald in the goal,
He saved shot after shot.
He dived around and caught the ball
And liked it quite a lot.

But then Gerald missed the ball,
Not saving like he should.
The ball went in, and so did he,
Head first in the mud.

So Gerald left the football team,
A postman he became.
"This mud is ruining everything,
It really is a shame."

He set off with his letters,
His bag full to the brim,
But a parcel was too big to fit,
So he knocked to see who was in.

Knock! Knock! He rapped, but no one came,
"They can't be in," he said.
But someone opened the door, knocked the pig to the flo
Straight into a flower bed.

This made Gerald unhappy.
"I'm doing the best that I can."
He thought he'd give it one last try,
"I'll be a fireman."

The engine he drove was big and red,
It sped along so fast.
"This is great! I've found my place!
I've found some fun at last!"

Gerald stood on his ladder,
Fighting fire through thick and thin,
But the ladder it broke and it's really no joke
When you see what he landed in!

So after all he'd been through
Gerald thought, "I just can't win.
It's not success that I land,
It's mud that I land in!"

Back he went and saw the farm,
His friends were all there too.
He watched them play, their faces smile,
And knew just what to do.

So maybe he wasn't a hero,
Saving goals or fighting a fire.
So he wasn't delivering important post
Or flying high on a wire.

But at last he is doing the thing he does best,
Not feeling little, but BIG!
Not trying to be something he knows that he's not,
He's happy just being a pig!

Roger

There once was a lion called Roger,
At hunting he was rather poor.
Whilst trying to pounce on his dinner,
He'd miss and fall on the floor.

But his wife enjoyed eating antelope,
So, in order to please her,
Instead of hunting he'd nip to the shop
And pick some up from the freezer.

Jigsaw

My grandma loves to do jigsaws,
She'll do them all the day.
Until she's finished the one she's on,
Nothing gets in her way.

She'll spread it on her table,
Sit with a cup of tea
And not move 'til it's completed
(Or until she has to pee).

The jigsaws are of anything:
A barn owl, a red setter,
A book, a hen, a duck, a pen,
The more pieces the better.

There's one particular jigsaw,
It's a picture of a deer,
She just can't seem to finish it,
She's been doing it all year.

It was Christmas when she started,
Slowly, bit by bit,
And now its late September
And she still can't finish it.

Every day and every night
The jigsaw will not end.
I think it's driving grandma mad,
She's going round the bend!

I can sometimes hear her in the night,
Cackling with the strain.
She'll throw the jigsaw on the floor,
Pick it up and start again.

I know why she'll never finish it,
But she won't hear it from me:
Two pieces were sucked up the hoover
And the dog's eaten at least three!

Big Thank Yous

Big thank yous to Ken and Heather 'Fingers' Walker, Patty-baby and Matty-boy (for Tuesday nights), Jo and Catherine, the Bennett's crew, Steve Rudd (for giving me a chance), Mr. Frost (my old English teacher) for fanning the flames, and Nic for keeping them burning.

As everybody knows, vampires can't really die.
It was just a flesh wound - I'll be back, by and by!